Dreams of a Viking Wedding

Dreams of a Viking Wedding

Poems by

John David Muth

Cover design by Shay Culligan

ISBN: 978-1-952326-11-0

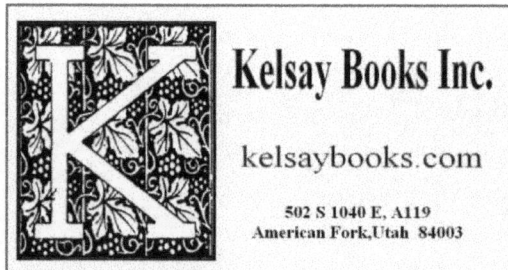

Kelsay Books Inc.

kelsaybooks.com

502 S 1040 E, A119
American Fork, Utah 84003

For Stephanie

Acknowledgments

Better Than Starbucks!: "An Apostate and a Heathen Try to Book a Church"

Eunoia Review: "How Many People Have You Slept With?"

San Pedro River Review: "She Does Not Know Her Wagner"

The Stillwater Review: "The Ninth Circle of Dating"

U.S. 1 Worksheets: "Pre-Wedding Jitters on the *Lusitania*"

Verse-Virtual: "Mop and Broom," "She Didn't Seem to Mind," and "A Sharp Piece of Wedding Cake"

Contents

Part I

Five Pills Every Wednesday

Five Pills Every Wednesday

I sit at the kitchen table
across from my father.
A wall of white bottles
stands in front of him like a firing squad.

Visibly annoyed,
he puts capsules into a row
of little plastic squares
marked for every day of the week:
blue, green, orange, pink,
medication to keep his cancer at bay.

Mom did this for ten years
up until she got sick.
Now dad has to do it
but I have to make sure he does it properly.

Writing out a check for the water bill,
I ask if the gas bill ever came.
He expresses his hope the gas lines rupture
blowing up the house with him in it.
I remind him to include his blood pressure pills.

Last year, my girlfriend, Emily, moved in with me.
We got engaged a month after this.
A week later, my mother died
much faster than expected.

I'm just managing to fill mom's shoes
but my greatest challenge
is the person who knew me best
the person who could fix any problem
isn't there to guide me
as I prepare to marry.

Ode to My 2-XL

I crawl through my father's attic,
look for things to sell
at a garage sale next week.
The narrow space and naked light bulbs
makes the place look like a mine shaft.

A dented box
with a robot on the front cover
sits on a cloud of pink insulation.
It was an educational toy
my parents bought for me
when disco was still popular.

Holding the plastic body
like Yorick's skull,
I remember the many hours
it quizzed me on math, history, astronomy,
how it got me to learn when I hated school:
the disinterested nods of child psychologists
and the subtle ridicule of teachers
dismayed I could not understand their lessons.
It never judged or criticized.
Even the dumb jokes it told were funny
when I was eight-years-old.

I plug the power cord into an outlet
hoping to see the red glow of its eyes
hear the high-pitched voice
ready to teach me once again
but nothing happens.
It must have been the heat up here.

The crash of dishes downstairs startles me.
Dad must have tripped over one of the boxes.
A surge of profanity
rushes through the hatch like a geyser.

I say goodbye to my little friend
thank him for his help all those years ago
yell to my father I'll be there in a minute.

Bonding at a Community Garage Sale

My father and I sit
in the middle of a long table,
its surface completely covered
with cat figurines and throw rugs
decorative baskets and metal utensils:
my late mother's possessions.

He glares as irreverent hands inspect
what once belonged to his wife,
runs his fingernails
over the denim of his jeans
when someone knocks something over.

My sister suggested we do this.
She said she would help.
The hospital gave her the weekend off
but they called her in unexpectedly.
Now she's cleaning vomit
and I'm listening to my father complain.
I really envy her.

He tells me most of the people here
are either fat or ugly
as I wonder who will get
my *Millennium Falcon* when I die
since I have no son
and my niece is not a geek.

An elderly woman
tries to haggle the price of a flower vase.
I have to refuse her offer.
My father's stare burns the back of my ear.
As she leaves, he says aloud:

Old bat probably has a million dollars
stuffed in the mattress at home.
She did not seem to hear him.

Ready for Work

My office once may have been
a crematorium for horses.
It's gray metal cold at 8 a.m.
smells a little like decay.
The light above me buzzes,
a psychotic hornet trapped in a bucket.
The congested cough
of a colleague next door
makes the wall we share vibrate.

The phone rings.
White particulates fall from the ceiling.
Deep within a carcinogenic daydream
I imagine Emily's dust and mine
floating in our empty bedroom,
sloughed skin from a scratch
fingers through sleep-tangled hair,
how they glow brownish gold
in the setting autumn sun
and dance in the forced air
of a recently repaired gas furnace
getting ready for our return.

A Message from the Provost's Office

I scan a conga line of work e-mails
consisting of angry students
and self-congratulating faculty.
There is also a new announcement.
We're getting another boss:
an Assistant Executive Associate Dean,
another link in the supervisory chain.

His picture reveals
a badly molded statue
of petrified cream cheese
in a nondescript, dark gray suit.
He smiles with his thumb up,
the best way of telling the world
he has not been self-aware since 1982.

My eyes fall on one of his several quotes:
I believe in giving students,
regardless of their background
the opportunity for personal empowerment.
I hope he feels the same way about his staff.

I look up his name online,
notice he had a bit of trouble
at his last university.
Three female students
graduated with substandard GPA's
after private consultations with him.
Coincidentally, his wife filed for divorce.
Subsequently, he left for health reasons.
I wonder if HR did any research on this guy
before offering him a six-figure job.
Of course they didn't.

A Normal Day at Bureaucracy University

It is the second day of fall registration.
A student prattles on about his future plans
while my mind's voice tries to drown out
his delusions of grandeur.

I have been advising students
for over twenty years
but no one has ever requested
a triple major in physics, law, and engineering.
We don't get many prodigies here.

You have a 2.3 GPA,
only slightly better than average
in the same way
stage 5 brain cancer
is slightly better than being dead.
Your desire to graduate in four years
is not going to happen
but I cannot tell you this
for fear of being reprimanded.

Who signed your permission form?
One signature is jagged
like a battlefield of spears,
the other is a wavy, horizontal line
like an ancient hieroglyph depicting water.
The dean from our office also needs to sign this.
Good. You can go after him
after your grades plummet.

Please stop talking and leave.
Once I obtain the signature
that confirms of my absolution,
your form will be processed.
If you try to contact me before this,
there will be no response.

She Worked Late Too

I come home late from work
see a trail of red
leading down the hall
drop my satchel
run to the bedroom,
hoping Emily
didn't cut a major artery
and bleed to death.

My dress shoes slip on the hardwood floor.
I slide into a decorative table
stab my thigh on a corner
land hard on my knee.

Trying to get up,
I notice the blood is really rose pedals.
She isn't dying.
She wants to be intimate.
It's been such a long time.

I limp the remaining length of the hallway
grab the doorknob
almost slip again
fling the door open
like a villain
in a poorly made spy movie.

She is lying on the bed
half-undressed
snoring,
one black pump still on
an open box of lingerie at her feet.
As my libido slips back into its coma,
I know that in only twenty short years
we will be helping each other
in and out of the bathtub.

Part II

How Many People Have You Slept With?

The Ninth Circle of Dating

The place is very cold.
Far below a precipice,
large black dots
wriggle on a field of ice.

This is a scene from *Inferno:*
21st century edition.
Middle-aged men and women
sit frozen in restaurant booths
try to converse through chattering teeth.
One couple stands on the dance floor
trapped in an embrace.
They argue about politics,
bite each other's faces raw.

I came so close to being there,
my right heel half over the ledge
my left planted heavily on loose soil
holding onto her
leaning forward
like we were dancing a tango
slowly shuffling back to safety.

I will do my best to make this work
try to listen when distracted
try not to take advantage,
raise shield or draw sword
(unless she really merits it).

Fear and love can live in symbiosis
and whenever we get the urge
to fly free of each other
I hope we remember
that elation
like a running jump from a cliff
only lasts a moment.

Backhanded Compliment

It's New Year's Eve in Soho
and we are walking to the apartment
of one of her friends.

Emily and I
have been together for two years.
In four months,
this will be my longest relationship.
I am glad it's still happy,
that the urges to leave her
in a desert with a broken foot
have been infrequent and of short duration.

A very drunk man
sits on the steps
of what might be his home
looks at Emily
looks at me
holds up a bottle of scotch and says:
I don't know how you pulled it off, guy
but good for you.

I thank him as she laughs,
not quite knowing
if he just saluted my prowess
or expressed disbelief
I could be with someone like her.

Learning to Drive in New Jersey

I sit in the passenger seat of my car
watch my fiancée start the engine
nervously clutch the steering wheel.

She's been living with me in central New Jersey
for well over a year.
Ten years in New York City
and a new job now necessitates
re-learning how to drive.

As we approach the nearest highway,
I impart my native wisdom:
Unlike New York
we never stop for pedestrians
so if you see one crossing the street
keep driving.
They will usually get out of the way.

When two lanes merge,
you can slow down to let a car pass
unless they drive a BMW.
In that case, hit the gas
even if the driver
is a pregnant woman screaming from labor pains.
Don't feel guilty.
BMW drivers are usually assholes.

Use your horn frequently.
If you need to use your middle finger,
make sure the windows are up
so if they hurl a projectile at you
it will bounce off the glass.

Mosquito Repellent

Men stare at her when we go out.
Some gawk like they are watching a movie
pretend I am invisible.
She tries not to notice.

A few margaritas with her girlfriends
might inspire playfulness,
a vivid recounting of pick-up lines
usually awkward and ill-timed.
She searches my face for annoyance
but I'm no amateur to this game.
Jealousy is the least attractive kind of insecurity.

She starts a new job next week
promoting a line of gym apparel.
She'll probably be working closely with salesmen:
glib and confident
fake Alphas in cheap suits.
There's a luxury suite in hell for them
one floor up from human traffickers
and people who beat their elderly parents.

She can handle herself
but I don't want to leave her unprotected.
I send a picture of me to her phone
from my days as a medieval reenactor
covered head-to-toe in armor
cutting watermelons in half with a sword.

I suggest she use it to scare off
the more aggressive misogynists.
If it doesn't work,
she can have one of me at the gun range.

How Many People Have You Slept With?

Emily asks me how many women
I was with before her
and I reply
enough to operate
a mid-sized aircraft carrier
including the flight crew.

She asks me again
and I reply
the women I have bedded
could each have their own seat
in a 1973 Volkswagen Beetle
and still have room
for an end table and lamp.

A patronizing laugh
tries to hide her impatience
but I know an answer
will invite another question.
I don't want to recount
my time with other women,
share intimate moments
of happiness and tragedy.
Our relationship
will see enough of both
in the coming years.

I suggest to her we treat our past lovers
like the 1920's pornographic movie
my best friend gave to me
as a joke for my thirtieth birthday.
We know it's there
but there is no need
to watch the movie together
as one of us has seen it
and the other is likely
to be bored or repulsed.

It Was Supposed to be a Nice Evening

She whispers,
teasing the hair in my ears
with her breath
tells me all the things
she wants to do to me tonight.

This is the second anniversary of our first date,
a night out at an upscale restaurant,
the overture to an opera
where the lovers die from mutual exhaustion.

A young couple enters the dining room,
probably BMW SUV drivers.
A pale-faced boy walks between them
holding their hands.

They're here to celebrate
little Zachary's graduation
from the first grade,
his ground-breaking research in napping,
his innate ability
to aim correctly when he pees.

His mother rattles off
his food allergies to the waiter
and many other ailments unrelated to food.
The boy loudly asks for chicken nuggets
in a place that serves
boar shank and quail eggs.

His parents converse
about whether to enroll him
into Aztec pottery making
or no-contact sabre fencing

while the child endlessly repeats
a greeting in Mandarin Chinese.
Emily tries to keep my attention
squeezes my hands as I imagine
shooting pine nuts dipped in gluten
into his oversized mouth
to see if his allergies are real
or just another example
of Munchausen syndrome by proxy.

Mop and Broom

This is an epicenter of the first world:
a wine and hors d'oeuvres soiree
hosted by the Ninth Bank of Manhattan.

A multitude mills around the old museum
holding wine glasses,
middle-aged
dressed for worship
though some look like
they got out of bed
mowed their lawn
and ran here without showering.

I am my fiancée's guest,
the financial beta of our union
listening to a jazz band
while she talks to a branch manager.
My bank never invited me
to anything like this.
I can't even get
an e-card on my birthday.

I lean against a wall
trying to eat from a fist-sized plate.
Dropped forks ring out reminders
my father spent forty years
cleaning up after people.
His mop and broom
put me through college
allowing me to blend
uneasily but almost convincingly
with such sophisticated company.

Putting the Brakes on a Verbal Argument

I tell her she is messy
leaves every room in disarray.
She replies I am neurotic
with unrealistic expectations
and breaks a chair over my back.

Straightening my spine,
I retort that the difference
between her and a pig
is a pig squeals less frequently
and I hit her in the temple
with a brass candle holder.

She looks at me
tilts her head from side to side.
Her neck crackles
as she ridicules my salary and my penis.
A knife slashes me across the face
while a knitting needle
simultaneously punctures my groin.

I pull out a small derringer
click back the hammer
ready to mention
her alcoholic sister
the ex-boyfriend who gave her
the scar by her ear.

But instead of shooting her, I pause
and remember some things
cannot be taken back.

I inform her my salary and penis,
while not enormous

are perfectly adequate
and walk away.

Talking with Grandpa after He's Had Ten Beers (circa 1987)

You kids don't know
how good you have it
with your paper-thin latex.
In the 40's, our condoms were so thick
they could be used again.
I had to fake my orgasms.
Your grandmother wasn't fond of them, either.

Then again, she didn't like sex very much,
so try to imagine dry rubber
trying to penetrate an unenthusiastic woman.
I suggested we do without
but after your father was born
she refused to have unprotected sex
ever again.

Never marry a Catholic girl, John-John.
Sex is a crucifix to their vampire.
Truthfully, they're all vampires.
Stay single forever
and remember
grandpa will always love you
even if you're gay.

Bread Causes Highway Hypnosis

Emily commandeers the radio
whenever we go on a trip,
loves music from the 1970's,
Todd Rundgren and Graham Parsons
musicians barely known
to younger generations.

The Adirondack Northway
is quiet north of Lake George,
few rest stops and not many cars.
She passed out
halfway through *America's* greatest hits.

Bread is the next band on her playlist,
sonambulist kings
and the first song is their crown jewel:
    If a picture paints a thousand words...
An invisible hand tries to close my eyes.
The surrounding countryside is so peaceful.
    If a man could be two places at one time...
It is getting rather difficult
to stay between these long, white lines.
    If the world should stop revolving
    spinning slowly down to die.....
Keeping my eyes fixed on the road
I try to find a song
from *Deep Purple* or *Led Zeppelin*
so I don't fall asleep
launch us off of this mountain.
    Then you and I would simply fly away....

Vespers at Weston Priory

On my annual pilgrimage to Vermont,
I take my fiancée to a Benedictine monastery
sitting on the edge
of the Green Mountain National Forest.

We wander the gardens and fields until dusk
make our way to a barn
illuminated by candles.
Several others come in and take a seat,
wait silently for Vespers.

Eight gray-haired men enter
wearing jeans and sneakers under their habits.
Two carry guitars.
They play while the others start to sing.

The hymns to nature and devotion
heighten my awareness of transience
make me think of my mother
and the old friend who first took me here.
My eyes blur as the sun sets.
I start to sniffle
tell Emily my allergies are acting up.
She takes my hand
knowing well I am a terrible liar.

After the service,
she jokes I should retire here.
It would be nice to spend
my last years as a monk

tending the greenhouse or harvesting honey
were it not for this atheism
and the fact I've grown accustomed
to fighting her for blankets
in the middle of the night.

Enduring the Dog

A few minutes after his walk,
my fiancée's dog peed on the kitchen floor.
Since she is out shopping
I have to clean up the mess.

He's lived in my home for over a year
but we never bonded.
He does not want to share her attention.
I do not want him in my territory.
Our feelings are irreconcilable.

We never had dogs when I was a child.
It was hard being allergic to everything,
always sickly:
head colds, tonsils, adenoids
ear tubes that left scars,
the possible cause of my tinnitus.
Though my fortitude developed,
my desire for a pet never did.

Why do people like dogs so much?
They are needy and high maintenance
always want attention
get distressed when left alone.
These are detestable qualities in a person
but I can always tell a person to piss off.

Admittedly, I do thank him for one thing.
He has revealed the depth
of my feelings for Emily.

I never would have endured
walks in the pouring rain
and picking up shit
had I only liked his owner.
Real love stretches patience
and forces tolerance.

Perhaps, when he takes that trip
to the Rainbow Bridge
I can convince her to get a cat.
I can probably handle a cat.

Part III

An Apostate and a Heathen Try to Book a Church

She Does Not Know Her Wagner

She loves the *Wedding March*
first practiced it when she was seven
did it for real
but with the wrong man
at twenty-five.
Now, at thirty-eight
she wants to do it again with me.

I mention absent-mindedly
it's from an opera by Wagner.
A brave knight appears
on a boat drawn by a swan,
marries a beautiful lady.

Emily smiles
until I tell her
the lady betrays the knight.
He then leaves her and she dies of grief.

Luckily, decades of bachelorhood
have acclimated me
to dead silence and cold dinner.

Our Preliminary Wedding List

I have no desire to see
Uncle Amos and Aunt Flo,
both of them over 90-years-old
shuffling through the *Electric Slide*
at my wedding reception
while the rest of the family
cheers them on.

Uncle Amos is an angry drunk
and Aunt Flo never forgave me
for a comment I made
right after my Confirmation
about how sexually frustrated
Saint Joseph must have been
being married to a virgin.

Without Amos and Flo,
we can drop their kids
Charlie and Rena
and their kids, Nina, Becca and Charlie Junior
and Charlie Junior's son
Zachary Charles.
The kid is only five-years-old
but will probably be an asshole
just like his father, grandfather and great-grandfather.

The list drops from 80 to 60 to 40.
I slash through names with glee.
Emily nods in agreement,
once the bride of a giant wedding.
Some nights, she still writhes in bed
from nightmares about fluttering doves
and shrimp cocktail.

We end the list at 30 names
and my father will cross himself
when we tell him of our plans
evoke the name of my mother.
He'll say it will kill Flo and Amos
to not be invited.
I'll respond that this will be a bonus
to saving $40,000.

Too Much of an Imposition

Emily's girlfriend
sent us a wedding invitation and itinerary.
I read it to her
while she takes off her makeup.

The girlfriend and her husband-to-be
plan to marry in Mongolia
at the end of next month.
It will have a nomadic theme.

After landing in Ulan Bator,
the guests take a caravan
into the Gobi desert
spend the night in a yurt.
The next morning,
the bride and groom
approach each other on horseback
wearing traditional Mongolian attire.
They exchange vows while still mounted.
After the ceremony, the guests will enjoy
a meal of grilled yak, goat cheese and mare's milk.

I ask if this friend
who has given us five weeks notice,
and expects us to travel thousands of miles
is worth the thousands of dollars.
She pauses
just long enough for me
to drop the invitation into the trash.

It's possible she'll lose a friend
she might see twice a year
but, on the bright side
we'll save all that money
and have two less people to invite
to our own wedding.

Mozart or *NWA*?

Do we really need a wedding song?
The highlights of our relationship
lack the appropriate music.

A street performer played
the lacrimosa to Mozart's *Requiem*
the moment we first met.
I put a dollar into his banjo case.

That evening, we dined al fresco
at a quaint Italian restaurant.
Our first kiss was almost perfect
marred only by NWA's *Fuck the Police*
blaring from the speakers of a passing car.
Remember how we ducked under the table
when the tail pipe backfired?

The first time we had sex
My Fair Lady was on TV
but *Thank Heaven for Little Girls*
is too creepy
and I only watched the movie
in the hope of getting sex.

Do we really need a wedding song?
We can always use *At Last* or *Canon in D*.
I only hope that years from now
Highway to Hell never comes to mind.

A Sharp Piece of Wedding Cake

Emily pulls me into a bakery
specializing in wedding cakes.
A girl at the counter smiles
shows us a giant book of photographs.

I stand by my beloved's side while she browses
trying to share in her excitement
but these cakes are monuments to vanity:
three tier
four tier
five tier.
This one has Greek columns holding up each level.

She stops to coo over one
that measures nearly half her size,
pure white
wreathed with red and pink flowers:
a polar bear standing in a rose garden.
A plastic groom sits at the top.
I imagine him with pockets turned inside out
a hangman's noose around his neck,
his bride
three times wider than he is
inserting a syringe of insulin
into her thigh
just above the garter.

The girl tells me
couples often put a slice of cake
into the freezer
and eat it on their first anniversary.

I respond if our first year doesn't go so well
I can always impale myself with it
while it is still frozen.

That little comment
turned into a four-day argument.

An Apostate and a Heathen Try to Book a Church

I walk to my car
arm around Emily's shoulder
trying to comfort her
as she sobs into a tissue.

She loved the old Catholic Church:
late nineteenth century Gothic,
gilded cross on the tallest steeple,
thought it would be the perfect place for a wedding.

The parish priest granted us a meeting
asked us some very personal questions
frowned at every answer
said we could not get married in his church.

We had to be members of the parish.
We had to go to church weekly.
Emily is a divorced Protestant.
We live together in glorious sin.
I left Catholicism out of boredom
at the age of seventeen.

Remembering the old priests of my youth,
I ask if we can use the building
bring our own justice of the peace.
Before he can answer,
I open my wallet
say there might be a donation in it for him,
maybe a few bottles of good scotch.

He calls me an apostate
tells me to get out.
Getting up to leave,
I tell him the Unitarians
would have never given us this much shit.

Pre-Wedding Jitters on the *Lusitania*

The tuxedo store is a sharkskin desert
and I wander past the racks
fending off hyenas
who want to take
my inseam measurements.
My best man is useless,
flirts with a soccer mom
who is helping her son
find a suit for his prom.

It will be a small ceremony,
no bridesmaids or groomsmen
thirty people and a reverend
but she shook her head
when I dusted off my suit
got angry when I told her
wedding gowns were similar
to overpriced condoms:
Even if the evening was memorable
it could only be worn once.
This is what I get for my honesty.

How many men have put on these pants?
Did their marriages survive
erectile dysfunction or job loss?
I can almost feel their hopes and fears
in the Italian-labeled Chinese fabric.

She wants black with tails
a white bow tie and vest,
early twentieth century elegance:

a first class passenger
on the *RMS Lusitania*
who saw a torpedo
gliding toward the hull
but mistook it for a dolphin.

Something Old

She climbs into the attic
moves boxes and plastic bags
to find an old cedar chest.

The hand-carved heirloom and its contents
are precious to her
passed down from grandmother to mother.
She dragged them from Topeka
to a dozen apartments in New York City,
some of them without air conditioning
some of them ten flights up
without an elevator.

The old wood creaks as she opens the lid.
A sea of ivory and orange satin
glows from the light of an overhead bulb.
Her eyebrows cross.
The light must be distorting the color.
She scoops up the fabric.
Microscopic holes and tears
exponentially expand
as her mother's wedding dress
disintegrates in her hands.

She consoles herself with the thought
it lasted longer than her parents' marriage
and she now has a place
to store her extra dishes.

Eschew the Bridal Gown

Emily sits in the bridal store
half-amused
half-perplexed
trying to find the right attire
for her second walk down the aisle.

One dress she liked was worth
three mortgage payments,
another could remodel a kitchen
with enough left over
for stainless steel appliances
and a mahogany floor.

Half a dozen young women
closer to twenty than thirty
look at themselves in full-length mirrors.
Some sob uncontrollably
anticipating their wedding day.
Others are angry
bark orders or whine
to employees and family
about hemlines
or a lack of decorative lace.

Emily gets up to leave
resolved to pick a dress from her own closet.
Thoughts of her first marriage come to mind
filling her with nostalgia and regret.

If all the money spent on her wedding
had been invested in real estate,
she could have retired comfortably
by her fortieth birthday.

A Wedding in Hvalsey Church (1408)

I could not tell Emily about
the dream I had last night
for fear it would make her upset.

The day before, I read
the last written record
of the Norse in Greenland
was of a wedding:
two people joining
in the little church
of a dwindling settlement,
a settlement that disappeared
less than one hundred years later.

We were exchanging our vows
in a candlelit room so dark
we could not see the walls.
I reflected on us
middle-aged
due to be childless,
saw my father and my best friend
widowers
ill and half-crippled,
our friends, like us
older, unmarried
or married without children.
Only my niece
thirteen and effervescent
gave me hope
we might live on in memory
a few more decades after our end.

I wondered if those hardy people
felt the passing of their world
and if that celebration
brought a distracting flicker of joy
to yet another Arctic night.

Part IV

A Cold Cannot Stop This Marriage

She Didn't Seem to Mind

I arrive a few minutes before
the concert is to start
enter the bathroom
and quickly head for a stall.
Urinals make me uncomfortable.
Other men always want to talk.
Some of us just want to pee.

This should be a good performance:
Berg's Violin Concerto
and Orff's *Carmina Catullus*.
My only concern is being seated
next to a cougher.

Leaving the bathroom stall,
I see an old woman washing her hands
and scowl at her senility
until I notice there are no urinals.
In the year since I've been here,
they made the men's room the ladies' room.

Tempering my panic,
I walk very softly
hoping she will mistake me for a woman
or ignore me completely
but I am six foot five in a black jacket,
a giant vulture perched on a 1950's TV
that throbs with static.

She looks up
her reflection in the mirror
like a starter pistol.

I run to the exit, explaining and apologizing
imagining handcuffs and fingerprinting
being put on a watch list
for sexual predators.

As I dart through the door, she says:
Don't worry about it, honey.

They Still Serve Meatloaf in 2047

I volunteer for many causes
because it's fun to pretend
one man can make a difference
that money and power
like a marble Janus
will one day care about
what I want and think.

Emily and I
dig holes in a nature preserve
put root bundles into soil
squirming with worms.
The work makes me think
about the future,
how we will shuffle
through this young forest
thirty years from now
married and happy
trying not to trip
and shatter anything important
enjoying the sounds of birds,
cursing at black flies
trying to drink
the moisture in our eyes.

Should zoning laws change
from the right hand being bribed,
I hope we are still together
sitting at this very spot
even if it means

eating meatloaf and open-faced turkey
every Wednesday at 3:30 p.m.
lamenting the summer of 2047
when they cut down the trees
and built a new *Denny's*.

Siberian Honeymoon

Where do we go for our honeymoon
when neither of us
likes people very much
especially the loud and fat kind
who enjoy conversing with strangers?

It should be a place
that does not remind us of home:
no gridlock traffic
no overpriced coffee shops on every block,
a place where we need not
pretend to be Canadians
in order to stroll unmolested.

We don't like the heat or water.
Our work schedules are busy
for most of the year.
I have narrowed it down
to Siberia or Iceland
between early January and mid-March.

Iceland is the better choice.
You are Danish and Norwegian.
I see the Viking come out in you
especially when annoyed.

Remember last week
when I referred to your girlfriends
as the Botox Brigade?
Those green moon eyes flushed red
like a bleeding warrior falling dead
into a pool of stagnant water.

You were cutting vegetables,
carrots and plum tomatoes
fixed your gaze to my groin
and repeated a saying
from your Jayhawk grandfather:
A gelded donkey rarely bucks.

Last Name Change

When we marry,
she is welcome to take my name
if she really wants it.
My family was never exalted
even when they lived in Europe
over a century ago.
They were mostly working people
and shopkeepers
with a sprinkling of vagabonds,
the smell of schnapps and cheap beer
gusting out from gaps in their teeth.

My thinking is not advanced enough
to take her last name.
Besides, her last name
belongs to her ex-husband.
That would be very strange.

She can certainly keep
her ex-husband's name.
He's a semi-tolerable person.
She wouldn't retain it from adoration
(that's for sure)
but from a strong reluctance to change
her driver's license
registration
passport
credit cards
bank account
social security card

retirement account
insurance
and investment information.
If things were reversed,
I would probably keep my ex's last name
even if I hated her.

What I Want Our Wedding Invitation to Say

Ms. Emily Edgar Martin
and Mr. Johnathan Cornelius Eindhoven
request the pleasure of your company
at their wedding,
about two months from now
at some kind of liberal church
or a nearby courthouse
as Johnathan believes organized religion
is a subtle form of mind control.

A reception will follow the ceremony:
probably a conveniently located restaurant
consisting of about thirty people.
Emily did the elaborate thing
for her first marriage
and it wasn't worth the cost.
Please indicate your choice
of chicken marsala or grilled salmon.
People with food allergies or dietary restrictions
should stay the hell home
so as not to ruin the fun.
On that note, leave your crying brats with a babysitter.

Cash is preferred in lieu of a gift
as they are hoping for a nice honeymoon.
They have enough junk in the house
and do not need more.

Please let them know if you can attend.
If you cannot,
save the bullshit excuses.
It doesn't matter.
They will see you another time.

A Visit from Mom

My deceased mother visits me in a dream
wearing her favorite terry cloth nightgown
and a dark green bathrobe.

J.E., do you really want to marry this girl?
Yes, mom. The sex is too good to give up.

Be serious. Why do you want to marry her?
We have many things in common:
a passion for mountains and forests
a need for creativity
a low tolerance for children
a barely contained misanthropy.

I ate too many Tastykakes when I was pregnant.
The sugar ruined your brain.
You need more than sex and hobbies.

I sit up in bed and look at her.
Her hands look like a 67-year-old's
but she has the face of someone ten years younger.

Mom, I respect her strengths and tolerate her flaws.
I trust her almost as much as I trusted you.
I'll be the best husband I can,
no bullshit fairy tales
just a man mature enough to persevere.

Her hard facial features soften.
You know you were an accident, right?
You turned out well,
but you started out as an accident.

Yes, Mother.
Had you only gotten pregnant two years later.
Roe vs. Wade could have helped you out.

Goodbye. I'm going now.
Bye, Ma. No one ever looked out for me
better than you.

A Bachelor Party Dungeon Crawl

I do not need a stripper
pretending to be a policewoman
ready to arrest
before the blatantly obvious reveal.

I do not need a hooker
with more tattoos than a Japanese yakuza
staring at the ceiling
imagining her next heroin fix
while she pretends
I'm giving her pleasure.

I just want to be a wizard
and play *Dungeons and Dragons*
for twenty-four hours
lightning swirling around my hands
blasting orc armies to pieces.
My friends will be at my side:
Ox and Morgan
Stevie and Brian
fighters, druids, barbarians, rogues.
There will be pizza, beer, whiskey and mead.
My intended will stay with a friend that night.

It's hard being inconsequential:
a machine that works, eats, excretes.
For a day, I want to be a warrior
passionate and fierce
not a white-collared geek
born a thousand years too late.

And when the last epic battle ends,
let them put my body
on a ship with all my treasure
light it on fire and set it adrift
toward the underworld
my remaining bachelor friends call marriage.

Wedding Bells Hurt When You are Hung Over

I see her through a crack
in the bathroom door
using the toilet as a pedestal
to shave her legs
as water from the tub faucet runs full blast.

Her hair is tangled
eyes half-closed,
the smell of secondhand smoke
drifts off her body
like flakes of skin from a funeral pyre.
It must have been
a wild bachelorette party.

She came in late last night.
I was in a deep sleep
but had recurring dreams
of being trapped in a burning vodka distillery.

Looking down the hallway,
there are boxes and bags
piled on the couch:
gifts from her girlfriends,
probably penis toys
and lingerie that would make
a whore from Amsterdam blush.
(I am rather curious about the latter).

Today is our big day
and I have to get ready, as well.
Walking back into the bedroom,
I admit the superstition
about not seeing a bride before her wedding
actually has some merit.

A Cold Cannot Stop This Marriage

We decided to forego the church wedding
the bridal gown and tuxedo
the limousine and banquet hall.
I drive my bride-to-be to the courthouse
in a newly-washed Nissan.
We'll have our reception at a nearby restaurant.

Before the judge
we pledge to do our best
put on gold rings
to mark our territory
hope we can work out big things
watch that the little things never snowball.
We love each other enough to try.

As we kiss to seal our oaths,
I notice my mother, grandmother, and grandfather
at the far end of the courthouse
suffused with blue light:
a scene from the end of *Return of the Jedi*.
My grandmother waves to me.
My grandfather reads a racing form.
My mother gives me a familiar gesture
about whether I have fresh breath.
I squint my eyes and crinkle my nose.
She smirks and shakes her head.

I may only be imagining
they have come from the afterlife
to wish me well.

I felt a cold coming on this morning
and took four Dayquil before we left.
Whether my dearly departed
are really here or not,
someone will have to drive me
to the reception.

A Fifty-Year Friendship

We hold our wedding reception
in the upstairs of a restaurant
that was once a nineteenth century farmhouse.
A dozen friends and family
converse in groups of two or three.
My father sits by himself
drinking a can of beer.

His hair is still black at 70
but his body aches are palpable.
A survivor of three kinds of cancer,
he is a World War II merchant ship
sailing onward
despite the holes in its hull
from submarine attacks.

He is missing my mother right now
and the sadness he tries to hide
almost makes me glad
I will unlikely feel that kind of loss:
the end of a 50-year marriage,
to know how hard it is to fly a helicopter
with the tail rotor missing.
I came to my relationship in middle age.
A seedling that fell from the wing
of a passing bird of prey
grew into a knotty mountain tree.

His best friend since high school
sits next to him
sees me observing them and points.

I don't know what he says
but it's usually something mildly insulting.
They laugh as I shake my head
and being the butt of an unknown joke
is worth seeing the shadow
fall from his shoulders
even if it's only for the evening.

About the Author

John David Muth is a lifelong resident of central New Jersey. He has been an academic advisor at Rutgers University for nineteen years. In his spare time, he enjoys hiking, road trips, and volunteering for environmental causes. He is a member of the U.S. 1 Poet's Cooperative. His work has appeared in such journals as *Better Than Starbucks!, Verse-Virtual, Muddy River Poetry Review,* and *U.S. 1 Worksheets.* He is the author of four collections of poetry: *A Love for Lavender Dragons* (Aldrich Press, 2016)*, Inevitable Carbon* (Aldrich Press, 2017), *Odysseus in Absaroka* (Aldrich Press, 2018), and *Reassure the Phoenix* (Aldrich Press, 2019).

www.ingramcontent.com/pod-product-compliance
Lightning Source LLC
Chambersburg PA
CBHW022015080426
42733CB00007B/611